2002 Presidential Award Winner
Best Business Title
Florida Publisher's Association

"This book hits the nail on the head! This book takes a topic (change management) that can sometimes be too abstract for most people to really understand, and uses humor and common sense to explain it in its simplest terms."
Jodi Littlestone, VP Human Resources

"Finshed the book on Saturday and read it again on Sunday. **I'll read Chapter 10 once a week!**"
Jeff Roider, Engineer

"Required reading for every change management (team) initiative in corporate America.
A practical and usable guide for ensuring the "sow's ear turns into a silk purse!"
Peg Lewin, Business Consultant

"**[The] book is a hit.** It has been a page burner for just about every employee."
Keith Callahan, Vice President, Materials Management

"**...it was excellent!!** I really enjoyed it and read it quickly! —it really is an awesome book!!! It was great and believe me, I too have encountered many pig snouts, boars and deal daily with angry sows. The difference now will be, as I sit in meetings, conference calls etc. and see these "piggish"behaviors, instead of getting frustrated I will just chuckle and move on."
Chris Yule, Sales Manager

"**I loved the book!**...the whole thing was very clever!"
Gwen Pinkerton, Executive Assistant

Provide your comments to this book to:
info@lessonsinpigfarming.com
We'd love your feedback.
We'd also like to hear about the challenges you experience while working in your "pig farm"

Lessons
In
Pig Farming

A Swine Farmer's Guide For
Surviving in Corporate America

By Cathy Sumeracki

Lisa?
I aspire to
your sense of
fashion
Be Great

Red Cabin Press

For book information contact:
Red Cabin Press
8659 E. Fillmore St. Scottsdale, AZ 85257

Or visit our website
http://www.lessonsinpigfarming.com

ISBN: 0-9716792-1-5

Library of Congress Number: 2002090709

Lessons in Pig Farming, A Swine Farmer's Guide For Surviving in Corporate
America, 2nd Edition
Previous ISBN: 0-9716792-0-7

Notice: Experiences on the pig farm are relayed solely from the author's
perception and do not necessarily reflect or represent any standard
practices. This book is not intended as a pig farming manual, nor is it meant
as a reference for large commercial swine operations. The author and Red
Cabin Press disclaim all liability.

PRINTED IN THE UNITED STATES OF AMERICA

*To Rich, who once said to me,
"Cathy, this pig farming
experience will affect your life."*

*And to Hunter, Rocky,
and the rest of the crew at
Gilt Edge Farms*

Lessons in Pig Farming
Table of Contents

Author's Note

This book is based on real experiences, both at the pig farm and through my experience at various large companies. However, I have used a writer's creativity to develop a story that is entertaining as well as informative.

Although the characters I have used are all based on real people, all names are fictitious with the exception of Pops in the last chapter.

After graduating from college, I had the opportunity to work on a large swine operation in Illinois. Ironically, it was there that I was first introduced to computers, which eventually led to a corporate career in the implementation of new programs.

I left the farm after 18 months and had filed it under "great Midwest experiences," never thinking I would use it again. However, after years in corporate America, I realized I hadn't moved very far from the farm after all. The lessons I learned in pig farming provided the foundation for me to survive in corporate America.

I'm not in coveralls anymore and I haven't worn rubber boots in years, but I am still moving sows and processing pigs. I still have to be careful around the boars, hit those angry sows head on and patiently deal with the pig snouts.

And I still need to be reminded that, in the end, it's all just pig farming.

Enjoy!

1

There's Always a Pig Snout

pig snout (noun) – pig 'snaut : 1) a pig's nose; 2) (slang), the one person who does not agree with the rest of a group

I followed the neatly landscaped path to the 101 building, heading for the employee entrance. The sidewalk was lined with tall, brightly colored red flowers like a line of tiny soldiers standing at attention, each welcoming me to the home office. Very fitting, I thought to myself, since most of my days were a never-ending battle.

I was part of the home office, a melting pot of 400 employees from different areas of expertise. Our function was to support and standardize the business processes of 60 or so facilities dispersed throughout the United States. (I say 60 or so because new facilities were added, sold or closed daily so it was never really clear how many there were on any given day). The company had been around for over 100 years, growing primarily through a series of acquisitions and mergers. For years, individual facilities had been free to run their own businesses. That was, up until now when the home office was created and began invading facility territory.

In "the old days" (as I am frequently reminded) each facility was free to do what they wanted, making decisions based on their individual needs rather than the needs of 'the whole company.' Now, with little warning, here come a group of yahoos from the home office (myself included) telling them how to run their business. This was the basis for my daily battle.

I saw both sides.

In defense of the home office, times *had* changed. The need for centralized processing and standardization was no longer an option, but now a necessity to remain competitive and ultimately, remain in business.

In defense of the facilities, I understood their frustration and resistance to change. After all, they had done quite well without us for years. In addition, the way changes were implemented always seemed to be rushed, without explanation and "effective immediately." (Eventually, I grew to *really* empathize with their position, but at this point, I was just another yahoo).

I worked in the purchasing department where we were implementing a purchasing program as part of a new "strategy." The overall concept of the new program was simple: centralize the purchase of supplies to take advantage of volume discounts.

However, like any other simple concept, its actual implementation turned out to be very complex. Century-old supplier relationships would be broken, new computer systems would be introduced; performance would be measured. Traditional processes the facilities had used and depended on for years, were all going away.

At the door I ran my employee badge across the security pad and waited for the green "go" light so I could enter the building. Once inside, I headed for the elevator to get to the fourth floor. Not that the fourth floor looked any different from the others. Each was a series of greenish gray cubicles of different shapes and sizes depending on work type and, of course, it's residents' level in the food chain.

During my first few weeks of employment, I used the stairs and once made the mistake of going to the third floor. Like a scene out of the Twilight Zone, I was confused by why everything looked exactly the same but the people looked different. For nearly 15 minutes I walked around the floor trying to navigate my way back to my cubicle before someone asked what I was looking for. They then pointed me to the elevator and told me I was one floor short. Since then, the elevator has been my landmark for orientation.

As a team member, (i.e., smallest box in an org chart) my desk was one of four surrounded by three and a half walls. This is also referred to as a "pod." Hard walled offices were rare, reserved for those whose title ended in "V.P. " or better. Everyone else lived in a cubicle. As you made your way up the ranks, you would get larger cubicles, perhaps even a higher wall and space for a table and chairs.

Despite it's challenges, I believed in the home office quest and loved being a part of the change. My boss, Dave Wilkes, Purchasing Team Leader , was another plus. We had hit it off in the interview and our connection continued to mature in the short time I'd been there. Dave's experience and calm management style were the very things I needed to counteract my passionate, emotional, go get 'em way of doing things.

As soon as I arrived at my desk, I turned my computer on so I could check my calendar. This was a daily routine I had adopted since my life seemed to be an endless string of meetings. I checked my watch. Today started with a nine o'clock project team meeting followed by a ten o'clock with Dave and then nothing until after lunch. Realizing I would have time to come back to my desk before lunch, I dropped my things, grabbed my notebook and headed for the project meeting.

I wasn't looking forward to this meeting. Seven of us met weekly for collaborative planning. The cast included my three other pod mates in purchasing, two team members from the Project Management Group, one team member from the Systems Development Group, and me. We were in the project development stage. This is where nothing gets decided before at least sixteen meetings, several heated discussions and majority vote from Congress. Prior to this development stage, we had surveyed the facilities to gain an understanding of what they were currently doing. This included questions about what they were buying, the prices they paid, the systems they were using, current processes, etc. We thought this would be beneficial but were disappointed. Many surveys were incomplete, some never turned in and others bearing information so far from reality, they could have been a fiction novel. Undeterred, we forged ahead.

Our meetings to date (this one being number five) had been marginally productive at best. Each had the same script. We would agree on a plan and begin to fill in the details when the infamous Greg Miller would argue some minute point until the rest of us couldn't stand it anymore. I was the last to enter the room and wasn't surprised to see Greg already engaged in a discussion with the other attendees.

"I'm just saying the surveys indicated the closest facilities are not the highest volume spenders. We should get the most bang for the buck and get as many savings as possible." Greg protested, talking to the group with his arms folded tightly across his chest.

Glancing down at the agenda in front of me, I saw today's meeting was to determine the first target sites for change. At the last meeting this had been unresolved. The rest of the group wanted to start with those facilities closest to the home office so we could be much more accessible if things went wrong. Greg saw this as a cop out and wanted to start with the largest-spending facilities.

Thankfully, someone made the suggestion to table the issue and move on to the next item before we ran out of time. I personally thought Greg ought to put a sock in it but in accordance with the laws of collaboration, we had to talk each topic to death before making any decision.

We moved through the rest of the topics then returned to the 'who should be first?' discussion. Not surprisingly, time ran out before the issue was resolved. Dave saw me exit as he headed for our meeting room.

"How'd it go?" He asked.

I rolled my eyes. Dave smiled and nodded towards the room we usually met in. "I'll meet you there."

When I arrived in the room, I closed the door and began talking as we sat down. "This collaborative process makes me crazy. I also know one guy who doesn't seem to get the concept. We talk, discuss, argue, make notes but can't seem to get him to agree on anything. An agreement would be a miracle - we could actually begin working! But oh no, Greg has to argue back and forth like it's the decision to launch a nuclear missile. To me and the rest of the group, as well as to all who would refer to themselves as sane, it's such a clear issue!"

I threw my hands up in exasperation. "We're never going to meet our deadlines if we can't make a decision!"

Dave was smiling, almost laughing.

"What's so funny?" I asked, looking up. His laughter agitated me. "And how come this kind of thing never gets to you?"

"Because it's just like pig farming," Dave said softly.

"Pig farming?" I blurted out, expelling a laugh. "How in the world is this like pig farming?"

"You asked me why it never gets to me and that's why. I went through everything you are going through now when I was on my first job - pig farming," Dave answered.

"You were a pig farmer?" I was still surprised. I just couldn't picture him slinging buckets of slop to a bunch of hogs.

"Oh, it's not what you're thinking." He must have read my mind, clarifying, "This was a *large* farm, over 18,000 head. We literally manufactured pork the same way other companies make a product. We had departments and sections, performance factors and measurements; new computers and software - we even had a consultant. You laugh but I didn't see the similarities until a few years ago myself. I was right about where you are now. New to the game, tired, frustrated - all of it. I thought about giving it all up.

Maybe take a job that didn't require any thought or just go live off the land somewhere. But then I realized this was nothing new. I'd gone through these same trials long ago but had somehow forgotten the lessons associated with them. I guess any good lesson is like that. You get it for a while then you forget it until it hits you right between the eyes. I thought my days at the pig farm were nothing more than a great Midwest experience. Once I learned computers, I left the farm and headed west. Life is funny, though. It always comes full circle. I learned some pretty important lessons on the pig farm - lessons that help me to survive here, in corporate America."

Still skeptical, I asked, "Like what?"

Dave tilted his head to the side. "Well, okay. What's the one thing that is upsetting you right now?"

I didn't hesitate. "Collaborative decision making. I understand the process but it certainly bogs down progress. It doesn't seem like decisions ever get made. And usually it's just one person holding up the process. Aaagh! It is a big waste of time."

Dave nodded. "Ah yes…the pig snout."

"The what?"

"The pig snout ," Dave repeated, now cupping his fist over his nose in a way that really did look like a pig snout.

Pulling his fist away, he continued. "See, on a large farm, pigs have to be moved from one section to the other depending on their stage of development. Pigs of the same weight and type all stay together. When it's time for the next phase, the pigs are moved in large groups into the next living arrangement. Literally, hundreds of pigs all moving in the same direction. You stand behind them and make 'ssshhhooosh' noises; each 'sshoosh' getting you a few feet forward. Looking over the top, it's like an ocean of pig rumps before you."

Dave paused, raising his index finger to make his point. "Except one."

"Always, at least one pig would be screaming to high heaven, fighting the tide, making his way back through the herd. You'd look before you and right in the midst of this open sea of pig tails, you'd see one little pig snout. It didn't matter how many pigs there were, how big; how old or how heavy, there'd always be that one little pig snout looking back at you. At first I'd be frustrated, just like you are now. Why doesn't this one get it? Then I got to where I'd anticipate the pig snout. Just that little shift in the thought process relieved my frustration. Then I developed a sense of humor about it. Sure, it made me work a little harder, think a little bit more but I actually came to respect the pig snout. If you think about it, that little piggy knew something the others hadn't caught on to."

"Kate, these endless meetings are really no different. Everyone will be moving in the same direction, driving towards a common goal but there will always be at least one pig snout, the one person who goes against the flow. There's always a pig snout."

"Okay, what do you do about the pig snout?" I asked.

"Same thing I did back then," Dave responded. "Most importantly, learn to expect it. That alone will ease your frustration. Then don't disrespect it but don't focus all of your efforts on getting that one pig to turn around. Work with it, understand it and where needed, create compromises. There'll be a pig snout in just about every group you meet with. You'll be the pig snout sometimes. We all are at one time or another. But, pig snouts are generally harmless and eventually they'll turn with the rest of the herd. Just like those pig snouts on the farm."

Involuntarily, I found myself chuckling. I guess it really was like pig farming.

Dave and I went through a few more items then ended the meeting. I left the conference room feeling better about the day. Returning to my cube, I thought about what Dave had said. To remind myself to expect disagreement as part of the process and to not take it so seriously, I pulled out a sticky note and wrote

There's Always a Pig Snout

and stuck it to my whiteboard.

There's
Always
a Pig Snout

2

Keep Your Head Out of the Pig Crate

*Pig crate (noun) – krate 1: an open box
made up of steel tubes or a usually steel
protective case or framework used to
house a pig; 2: (slang) other peoples'
business*

Over the next few meetings I watched patiently as Greg eventually understood the need to work first with facilities closest to us. In turn, the rest of the group understood the need to get as many savings as possible. A decision was made. The first group to change would be those geographically closest but the next wave would be those who had the largest spend. The herd was moving in the same direction at last.

Progress could be seen as we filled Microsoft Project timelines, pushed pins into maps and created countless spreadsheets of information. Now it was time to present our plan to other departments to be sure we were working together. This included Accounts Payable (AP), Information Systems (IS), and Systems Engineering (SE). For me, the lone soldier type, this meant more collaboration with more people. I just wanted to get started.

Weeks before, we had met individually with each of the departments to make sure we understood their needs. For example, we verified our coding system would be compatible with AP. We evaluated the computer needs with IS. The logistics of loading the software was discussed with SE. Taking this information, our core team then went to the drawing board and drew up a plan that would take into consideration all the needs of all of the various groups.

Dave joined us for this meeting.

Eight people were physically attending while five others joined us via teleconference. The black box sat ominously in the center of the table, periodically chirping as people joined in. Of course, every chirp was followed by a subsequent interruption to determine who joined in or who left. If someone were joining, the meeting would be summarized again and participants reintroduced for about the millionth time. One caller had to leave for a moment and put her phone on hold, filling the room with the Bee Gees. Between that and the guy who was calling in on his cell phone from rural Oklahoma, we were a good 15 minutes into the meeting before the first topic was introduced.

From the start, it was evident there were a number of shortcomings. We learned AP failed to inform us that there were actually *two* sets of accounting codes and the coding we presented would not be compatible with both systems. The IS group announced that because of firewall restrictions, we would have to visit each and every desktop to install software rather than use an internet connection. They explained it but I couldn't comprehend it. They also pointed out that many of the desktops in the field would have to have Windows upgraded before anything could be done. Adding with this last revelation that this required an additional "PAN" (Project Approval Number) and another five signatures before moving forward. The current backlog for PANs was three weeks.

The list wore on.

I was flabbergasted. I thought to myself, "When did they think of these issues?! These items should have been brought up when we met with them individually! Was that just an exercise? Why weren't these issues brought up *before* we spent the last 100 hours making up this plan?"

I noticed no one said much during the meeting except of course me, who immediately jumped in the second the room was quiet. I was filled with an abundance of ideas regardless of whose area. And I was quick to point out the best way for everyone to do their job.

I left no one unscathed.

I suggested accounting develop a spreadsheet which would include all of the codes so we could use this as a reference. I suggested the IS group rethink their plan and come up with a way to use the internet as we had originally intended. I suggested the SE group review the original PAN that was approved months ago and see if we could add to it without having to have it re-approved. I was on a roll.

Following each of my suggestions, a typical response from whoever's area would be "That's a great idea, Kate. Why don't you work us something up and at the next meeting, we can look at it."

Each response caused my teeth to clench. Do these people actually get paid to work here?

By the end of the meeting, I was overloaded with projects, as well as an abundance of bad attitude and all the fixings for a pity party. The stress made my head feel like it was in a slowly tightening vise. I was glad Dave was there. He could see first hand how much work I was doing.

As we filed from the meeting room, I checked my watch. I had a lot to do so I headed for the vending machines to grab a soda and pretzels, a common lunch entree when things got busy. Dave caught up with me near the elevator.

"Want to grab some lunch?" He asked.

I checked my watch again. "I was just going to hit the vending machines. I don't think I have time today."

"Yeah, you did have a lot of projects added today." Dave got in the elevator.

I smiled at his comment. I could use more positive reinforcement. Knowing Dave would shower me with 'atta boys' to keep me going, I reconsidered lunch.

"Okay, if we hit Jerry's it'll be quick and my stomach will thank me."

Dave and I exited through the back door to take the short cut to the rows of restaurants behind our

23

building. Surprisingly, there was no line at the popular lunch café. Dave and I got our food right away and sat at a far table in the outside eating area. I waited in anticipation for Dave to comment on the meeting. When he didn't mention it right away, I prompted him.

"So, what did you think about the meeting today?" I asked, as nonchalant as I could muster.

Dave responded without looking up. "I think you volunteered yourself for a lot of work. A lot of work that unfortunately isn't going to mean much."

Stunned, I snapped back, "Not going to mean much- what do you mean? It's…it's the whole project!"

Still in the throws of self-pity, I added, "And I didn't volunteer, Dave. They gave me those projects. Who else was going to do it?"

"They were being polite, Kate." Dave looked at me now, his voice remaining low.

"Polite?" I said through a mouthful of sandwich. "What's that supposed to mean?"

Dave leaned forward in his chair now, and explained, "Yes, Kate, polite. What they really wanted to say was 'please stop talking Kate and mind your own business!'"

I was shocked. Here I was working so hard and a little appreciation would have been nice. I'm certain the scowl on my face reflected my resentment.

Noticing, Dave responded, "Kate, please sit back and hear me out."

I pushed my half finished plate aside. "Okay, I'm listening." I sighed. "You've got my full attention."

"Kate, I have a lot of years on you but it wasn't that long ago that I was just like you. Anxious to jump in wherever I thought I could help. And I jumped in just like you do. Right in the middle without giving much forethought on the outcome. I was a tough learner, but pig farming taught me a great lesson about not putting my head where it doesn't belong."

I couldn't wait to hear this. I put my elbows on the table now, resting my chin on one hand as Dave spoke.

"On the farm, we had over a hundred pigs born every day. That's about 10 sows per day going into labor. The well-being of the newly born pigs is critical so a lot of time is spent making sure deliveries go smoothly. Taka was a gentleman who worked with me in Farrowing, that's where pigs are born. Taka was from Japan and I learned a lot from him. He showed me a technique to use whenever a sow was having trouble delivering. What you'd do is crouch down close to the sow and rub her belly very gently. It took awhile but if you kept at it, eventually she'd calm down. Like magic, she'd lay down then pretty soon, a little piglet would come out."

"Well, late one night I was walking the barns by myself, looking for any signs of trouble. As quietly as possible, I walked up and down the aisles separating the three rows of crates. Pretty soon I came upon a little gilt. A gilt is a female pig that hasn't yet had a litter. Once she has a litter she is referred to as a sow. Anyway, this little gilt was really having trouble. She'd stand up, lie down, and stand up again. I was excited. I'd just learned my new belly rubbing technique and was eager to help."

"Now, one thing to keep in mind is a pig crate is built just big enough for the Mama pig. It's made up of a series of metal pipes forming an elongated dome shape around the sow or gilt. Like a long open igloo. Around the crate is a short walled pen, about six feet by six feet, the walls maybe a foot high. This is where the little ones run around. In order to get to the gilt's belly, I had to step into the pen and put my arms through the openings in the crate. As Taka had shown me, I put my hand through the side and tried to rub her belly. She just did not want me there. I tried a number of other positions but nothing was working. About the only thing she would tolerate was me leaning over the top of the crate and reaching my arm down through the opposite side. So that's what I did. It took awhile but to my amazement, she finally laid down. I was the regular midwife then. My confidence was high."

"Well, when she laid down, my arms couldn't reach her belly anymore. I was afraid to move back down beside her because I didn't want her to get upset again. So without thinking, I adjusted my position so I was still over the top of her but now my body was actually inside the crate. I continued to massage her belly."

"Now, I've already told you about the size of the crate. I'll also share with you that despite their comical appearance, pigs are really quite athletic and they are quick....very quick."

"So there I was, leaning inside this crate, gently rubbing the gilt's belly, not a care in the world except helping this little mama along. Suddenly, one of the other sows got up and banged against her feeder. In the silence of the big barn, it sounded like a cannon went off. In a millisecond, and I mean millisecond, that gilt was up on her feet. Not only was I still in the crate, but now the top of her back had my head cranked at about a 90-degree angle against the top steel bars. We were both scared to death. When I tried to pull my head out, she humped her back in fear, pressing my head further into the bars. If I stayed still, my back and neck felt as though they would break. I'm telling you, my life flashed before my eyes. I hung there for what seemed like eternity but it was probably more like two minutes.

Somehow, and I can't even tell you how, she finally relaxed enough for me to get my head out."

"In hindsight, I couldn't believe I had made such a stupid move. It was a tough lesson but a good one. Don't put your head where it doesn't belong! Keep your head out of the pig crate!"

By the time Dave ended his story, I was doubled over in laughter. As I wiped the tears from my eyes I was in a much better mood to see his point.

"So that's what you feel like I'm doing? Putting my head in the pig crate?"

"Precisely Kate. I know you love what you do, and I also know you could probably handle this project all on your own but there's not enough of you to go around. Besides, that's not what team building is about. You were hired for your expertise in purchasing and transition management. The other people in that meeting today were hired for their various areas of expertise. Good teams require everyone does their part - not just one person trying to do everything."

Dave continued, "What happened in the meeting today, the introduction of new information when you're nearly complete with the planning phase, is how projects usually progress. As more people understand the full scope, more issues arise. These are issues other groups didn't necessarily understand prior to this point."

I started to speak but Dave held his hand up so he could finish. "And this may sound harsh, but it isn't *them* giving *you* work. You volunteered for it. Just like it wasn't that gilt who nearly broke my neck. It was me who stuck my head in her crate in the first place. Kate, in that meeting today, you had all of the space sucked up, barely giving anyone a chance to talk. They don't want you to do their jobs anymore than you do – they just don't know how else to tell you to butt out!"

Dave's long intake of breath let me know he wasn't finished. I continued listening.

"Kate, if I had a hundred employees like you, I'd love it. You're intelligent, a quick thinker, and very efficient. But you also need to understand that not everyone works the way you do. Tone it down. Learn to ask questions rather than give orders. Focus on your own area and I think you'll be surprised at the progress the others make. It's your role to inform them about what you are doing and to point out areas where it may affect their departments. It is not your job to take on their roles or to tell them what to do."

Dave tapped my shoulder affectionately and smiled before rising, "Keep your head out of the pig crate, kiddo."

On the walk back to the office, I thought of Dave's story, still smiling at the thought of his head stuck in the pig crate. I also thought about the morning's meeting. I really had taken over without thinking about everyone else. I was too wrapped up in my own self-righteousness to understand how irritating I must have been. I was glad Dave pointed it out and I didn't want to forget it.

Back at my cube, I added another sticky note to the whiteboard:

Keep your Head Out of the Pig Crate

There's
Always
a Pig Snout

Keep Your Head
Out of
the Pig Crate

3

Always Factor in
the Sow Effects

Sow effect(s) – (noun-adverb) sow e' fekt:
1: the reaction(s) in a sow when changes
are made; 2: (slang) problems that reveal
themselves whenever a plan is
implemented, often coming as a surprise
to those who thought of everything.

Keeping my head out of the pig crate resulted
in a much more reasonable workload. In meetings, I
focused on my own area and learned to ask questions.
Meetings became much more constructive. Still a

few pig snouts here and there, but we were learning to work with each other.

Activity was at an all time high as we completed our first implementation. We were confident we had thought of everything. HA!

Twenty four hours post start time, the alarm sounded and continued through the week. Computers bleeped endlessly as emails filled our mailboxes. Pagers and cellphones sang a discorded electronic chorus. All the things we *hadn't* thought of suddenly exposed themselves.

The software wasn't working on any of the computers in shared central areas, pricing data was inaccurate, tax was calculating incorrectly. The major crisis involved the units of measure. Cases and cases of material were arriving at the dock when just a single item was ordered. Our team was scrambling to make corrections and create work arounds. We were working long hours to accommodate this new money-saving plan.

We all took a much needed break from the turmoil to attend the quarterly "we're here to pump you up" meeting. This is where highly paid consultants and top levels of management get together to share "the vision" and tell you how great everything is. Four hundred employees made their way to the cafeteria for the big show.

After a few introductions and a few jokes to get us in the right frame of mind, the meeting was turned over to the consultants. The consultants were the originators of the great vision. It was our job to make the vision happen.

Brightly colored slides and graphs filled the large screen at the front of the room, each revealing another step in the plan. Savings were printed in large bold print at the bottom of each slide. We'll save millions!

I was taken in by the enthusiasm but not quite sold. The backlash from the first implementation was still lashing and this was just the first. I couldn't imagine the problems awaiting us after we got through 25 or so. To listen to this guy, it was going to be so easy!

The last presenter was the most entertaining. After he finished, we thanked him with a large round of applause.

We'll save millions!

I met up with Dave as we filed out. I wanted to share with him how I felt, but I didn't want to come across as being negative.

"Isn't it crazy? It's taken so long to think of this when it's so simple?" I tried the sidelong approach.

"Oh, I don't think it's that simple. Certainly not here." Dave laughed now. "I noticed no one mentioned the 'sow effects.'"

"What do you mean?" I asked, knowing I was in for another lesson in pig farming.

Dave elaborated on our way to the fourth floor. "I see it all the time. People create plans that look great on the surface. Do this, do a little of that, boom – you save millions! It's amazing isn't it?"

We both chuckled. I was glad Dave felt the same way I did. I followed him into his cubicle and we both sat down.

Dave continued. "Believe it or not Kate, it was no different on the pig farm. That's where I first learned about sow effects. The consultant for the farm had this great plan to save big dollars.

I got comfortable in my chair and listened.

"Like this company, Kate, everything was about the bottom line. In pig farming, the bottom line means getting a pig to 230 pounds as quickly and as cheaply as possible."

"One of the major challenges of pig farming is to get all of the pigs born at the same time. When sows are brought over from Gestation, (that's where they're bred), to Farrowing, (where they'll give birth), the thought is the sows coming over have all been bred within the same week. If this is true, then they should all give birth in the same week. Pigs move in groups and the more uniform the group, the more efficient the farm is. Just like any product."

"Mother Nature isn't as cooperative. Some sows didn't give birth until two weeks after the move. Baby pigs gain about half a pound per day so these late bloomers would be way behind in the process. You didn't have the luxury of letting them nurse a few more weeks because the pigs move together. These younger pigs had to be weaned at the same time as those who were born first."

"Well, this consultant came up with the idea of giving all of the sows a shot to start labor when they entered the farrowing barn. This way, they would all give birth at the same time and the pigs would be all the same age when they were moved. It really is a great idea!"

"He would measure the success of this project by the amount of immunoglobulins that transferred from the mother sow to her pigs. Immunoglobulins are important antibodies the newborn pigs get from the sow's first milk, colostrum. He would induce labor in half of the sows by giving a shot of oxytocin and the other half of the sows would give birth naturally. If the amount of immunoglobulins were the same in the pigs coming from induced sows as they were for the pigs coming from sows who gave birth naturally, the project would be a success. We'll save millions!"

"Well, the research period lasted six weeks. As each litter was born, blood was taken to measure the amount of immunoglobulins."

"For me and Taka, this was six weeks of chaos. Typically, births occur with little difficulty, but now we saw many problems. Sows blissfully waiting the big day were suddenly thrown into hard labor, resulting in a number of stressed sows. They panted; they went off feed. It was just a mess. Gilts were the worst. Excess straining left them tired and irritable. They were less apt to pay attention to the new piglets. All of these effects are what I call 'sow effects'. Because of the sow effects, Taka and I worked long hours, accommodating this 'timesaving' technique."

"At the end of six weeks, the results were in. I was sure it wasn't going to be a success. It'd been too difficult. But would you believe those tests came back and they showed no difference?! Immunoglobulin levels in pigs coming from induced sows were the same as those who gave birth naturally. Success! We'll save millions!"

Dave laughed to himself then concluded the story. "Thankfully, the consultant did concede that though the results indicated success, other factors would have to be evaluated before conclusions could be drawn. He was not ready to start the marketing campaign – Whew."

"Kate, this project is full of sow effects. Anyone can show where savings are but you and I both know there is no such thing as a simple solution when it comes to change. The connectivity issues you're having, the changing of codes, the strong resistance - all of the things not shown on the colorful graphs - these are all sow effects. And sow effects can be hard to measure especially when they're the emotional effects of change. Confusion, anger, misunderstanding- all sow effects. Sure, the concept of centralization is a simple one, just like giving a shot to have sows deliver pigs at the same time is a simple one. The sow effects are what make it difficult. You plan carefully to minimize sow effects but they'll still be there. Your plan should allow space for them. The bottom line is savings yes, but other equally important factors exist and should be measured. The number of complaints, user satisfaction, the number of errors to name just a few. These are also good measurements of a project's success. The money saved is important but if you spend twice as much in labor to save the money, you haven't achieved anything. Solely looking at the bottom line does not necessarily show the whole picture."

Dave stopped talking allowing me to absorb all he'd shared.

"I can attest to that," I said with a sigh. "I thought about jumping in front of a fast moving truck after this first implementation. It's been crazy. But if sow effects just exist, how can we make it better?"

"You're right, some sow effects show up no matter how hard you plan but many can be reduced. That's the second part of the lesson, Kate. The first was 'Always Factor in the Sow Effects.' The second is 'Move Sows Gradually Along a Clear Path.' Let me take a little break for a second. I'll be right back."

While Dave was gone, I jotted a note to myself:

Always Factor
in the
Sow Effects

4

Move Sows Gradually Along a Clear Path

"Changing the direction of a large company is like trying to turn an aircraft carrier. It takes a mile before anything happens. And if it was a wrong turn, getting back on course takes even longer."
-Al Ries, Chairman
Trout & Ries Advertising, Inc.

While I waited for Dave, I pondered over the sow effects in our project. Technical problems were a big issue but I knew they were solvable. Other issues weren't as easy to overcome.

For one, the facilities hated us. Half the time I felt like I should drop my business casual attire for a t-shirt with a big red and white target on it and a caption reading, "Hi, I'm from the Home Office!"

I also discovered that any material sent out ahead of time is quickly absorbed in the thousands of other publications the facilities are expected to read and understand. On the rare occasions when material is read, many misunderstand the processes and much of our time is spent explaining what we were trying to explain in the first place.

People were flustered, short tempered and confused. I could make a fortune if I was paid per complaint call. All I had heard for the past 24 hours was, "I don't have time for this" and "It worked fine the old way!" Sow effects indeed. Yet none of these issues were discussed in today's meeting as issues. Just save, save, save those millions!

Dave returned and sat down across from me again. "When you're dealing with sow effects, Kate, you have to remember you're moving sows."

"I'll say," I interjected, "and are they heavy!"

We both laughed for a second before Dave continued.

"No, I'm serious, Kate. When we first talked about this change, I knew the culture here would be one of the major challenges. It'll eventually change, but you have to understand that people are confused and frightened by change. You're new here and don't have a long history of doing business the same way for years and years.

You know it's a good move and it'll be beneficial in the long run but they don't see it that way. I'm sure many feel they're being overridden and are no longer important. They're venturing into unknown territory and don't trust it. With all the pressure of you and everyone else at the home office telling them they *have* to do it, they're freezing up. This is exactly like moving sows."

Dave rolled his chair forward, excited to make his point.

"Remember I told you the sows had to be moved from the Gestation to Farrowing?"

I nodded, remembering.

"Well, once bred, the pregnant sows stay in Gestation until they're ready to deliver - about 4 months. To a sow, this is a lot of time to adjust to the routine and to know what to expect. They have a routine. They get fed twice a day, it's familiar. Then low and behold, one day we come into the barn, disrupt their daily lives and ask them to move. They don't want to move. Why move? Well, they have to move. They can't have pigs in Gestation. There's no room. They have to go to Farrowing where the accommodations are much better suited for their needs."

"Each week, a new batch of 60 sows were ready 'to pig,' that means give birth. This meant moving them to the Farrowing barn. This is where I worked so I was on the receiving end of this task. When I first arrived at the farm, the two guys in Gestation would move the sows at lightening speed. Sixty sows would be backed out of their crates and sent at a full gallop through the maze toward Farrowing. A typical route included a run down a narrow aisle and a couple of sharp turns before the path widened to an open aisle at the end of the Gestation barn. Here there was an open outside walkway between the two barns before entering Farrowing. Once in Farrowing, the aisles narrowed and split off into two separate rooms filled with crates. The crate was the final destination. It was quite a maze."

"Those 60 sows would be at a dead run by the time they reached the edge of the outside walk. Stunned by the light and sudden change in environment, they'd stop and jam up like a sold out crowd at a general admission concert. The two boys would catch up with them, hollering and making a racket to get 'em going again. The effect was like catapulting sows into Farrowing. They'd run over the top of each other, run over the top of us. It was crazy! Eventually we'd get the sows into their individual crates but certainly not before a lot of damage was done."

"First off, the barn was always a mess. Crates were torn from the floor, the short walls of the boxed area would be flattened and scattered. Metal feeders, normally anchored at the front of the crates, hung sideways or

were completely torn off after a run-in with a fast moving sow."

"Our crew was a mess. We were out of breath from the chaos and strung out from the adrenaline rush. Our hands had been jammed and pinched against the crates as we frantically closed the back gates as sows ran in. One guy broke his ankle when a sow ran over him."

"And finally, the sows were a mess. The first day in their new home was spent panting, stressed and exhausted. And remember, these were sows just ready to give birth!"

"When I talked to Taka about it, he agreed it was crazy but said, 'It's always same. Have to move sows fast.' I disagreed. I hated moving sows because I couldn't stand the way it was done."

"A few weeks later the boys were dazzling the lunch crowd with the latest 'running of the sows' story, pointing out how much time they'd saved. I used the moment to challenge them, asking about the time it took to clean up the mess and repair the damages.

Couldn't we try it differently to ultimately save time for everyone?

"Well, the hum of the lunch crowd went up, punctuated by 'oohs' and 'aaahs'. I was challenging *the way it's always been done.* How dare I? To make a long story short, it took a few heated discussions to finally get them to oblige but they agreed to try it a different way."

"In preparation, Taka and I got additional boards to clearly mark the path from one side to the other. Corners were blocked, doors closed, and driveways roped off. Nothing but the desired path remained. Before we started, I met with the guys from Gestation and asked for only ten sows to be brought out at a time."

"Of course, complaining and wisecracks erupted. They whined and hollered, 'we'll be here until next week!' But in the end, they backed just ten sows out. And there was no screaming and hollering - someone would walk behind the sows and *encourage* them forward."

"Well, the first ten were quietly put away. Minor adjustments to the path were made for the next ten and they too filed to their crates. This pattern continued until all 60 sows were in. We checked our watches – the new way actually took less time! It worked! Not a single casualty that day- no damaged crates, no employee injuries and no stressed sows. From then on, that's how we moved sows."

Dave smiled proudly then continued. "Kate, I remember that lesson more than any other. All too often I've seen corporations try to move people from one system to the next with lightning speed. Normally it's not with yelling and screaming but lack of communication can be just as damaging."

"Change is inevitable, that's a fact - but it doesn't have to be so painful. We beat change into people without taking the time to understand what they're doing now. We tell them what they're going to be doing from now on with little direction on how to get there. In our haste to save the big bucks we often bypass the education process, failing to explain how to change and why the change is needed. Without a clear path from where they're at now to where you're asking them to go, you get chaos. The same as it was in pig farming. Move things too quickly and you end up creating damage. Here, in corporate America, instead of damaged crates, we have damaged infrastructure. Instead of stressed sows, we have stressed employees. Many so flustered, they leave the company. And often leave at a time when we really need their expertise. Those who remain are often unmotivated, making future changes even more stressful. Communication breaks down. The company culture becomes 'us against them' when it should be all of us working together. It can cost valuable time and money to clean up the damage."

"And Kate, it's not like I think no one cares or that the people who gave those speeches today are really unaware. They simply minimize the impact change has on people. They ignore the sow effects. It's so easy to look at something from way up high and see the benefits of the end results. Getting *to* those end results is hard work. It's a convoluted maneuver to move people from age-old routines to standardized processes, no matter how much more improved or more simple the new processes might be."

I was nodding my head in agreement. I clearly understood Dave's point. He continued.

"If you can look at the change from the facilities' perspective and clearly show them the way - and I mean show them the way for them, not just how the home office sees it - this transition will go much smoother. Listen to their concerns, understand what they're doing now. This way, you'll know better how to get them where they're going."

Dave anticipated my concern about deadlines.

"And another thing, I know you've been focused on your deadlines Kate, but I'm suggesting you forget about the deadline just for a minute and instead evaluate the path you've created from what people are doing now to what they'll be doing in the future. Take the time to test all of the systems. Don't implement quickly just because it's always been done that way. Make a difference. Encourage people forward rather bully them into your timeline. Sure, they'll still hesitate. They're just like those sows hitting the edge of the open walkway. It's new, it's foreign and they're nervous. Allow some time for people to digest changes and they'll be more comfortable. Trust me Kate, with all of the time you save in damage clean up, your timeline will be just fine."

I liked what Dave was saying and I wholeheartedly agreed. In our efforts to save millions, we were moving much too quickly – or at least trying to. Many hours had already been spent correcting damage. We *were* costing the company more dollars although it wasn't necessarily showing up on any color graph.

I thanked Dave for the lesson and returned to my desk. I was motivated to make changes so we could minimize the sow effects.

In looking at the communications to the field, I put myself in their position and could understand why they were so frustrated. Much of the communication gave the end result but gave vague direction on how to get there. And it was clearly one sided- focusing only on what the home office needed.

Over the next week, our team met daily to re-evaluate our implementation plan. We could see where communication and education had been lacking. We adjusted the plan to allow more time for facility education and communication. We reviewed current facility processes more closely, asking more questions. From this we created more simplified process maps to help people navigate the transition. We developed contact lists and made phone calls to those who would be affected, making sure we understood their concerns before moving forward. We also created a monthly report showing the savings as well as measurements of other issues, including the number of complaints and the number of errors per facility. By monitoring some of the "sow effects ," we were not only able to show improvement, but were also providing reassurance to the facilities that their problems were being addressed and resolved.

At the end of the week, I added the two new lessons to my white board so I would remember to understand and allow for the effects caused by change. The second reminder I marked with a star to emphasize the importance of making changes gradually and with clear direction.

Always Factor in the Sow Effects

Move Sows Gradually Along a Clear Path

There's
Always
a Pig Snout

Always Factor
in the
Sow Effects

Keep Your Head
Out of the
Pig Crate

*Move Sows
Gradually
Along a
Clear Path

5

Remember to Include the Details of Pig Processing

"The understanding of instructions varies greatly between the one who is writing them and the one who is following them."
-Unknown

Improvement was noticed immediately in the next implementations. We were glad we had spent the extra time revamping the plan. Complaint calls receded to a manageable level. I no longer felt like hiding in the email bomb shelter after logging on to the network each morning.

The greatest improvement was in the attitudes of the facilities. Including them in the process instead of telling them what to do shifted their viewpoint. They still weren't completely sold on the new system, but the hostility was gone. Much of the anger was just plain frustration of not being communicated to. It was a welcome change for both sides. I saw it as an unspoken truce in the age-old conflict of "home office verses the facilities."

The project developed a healthy rhythm. The team continued working at an assertive pace but more positive feedback and less complaining kept enthusiasm high. We now had over 15 facilities completed and were juggling resources between implementation and the daily administration of the program. With so much to do, Dave agreed to hire an administrative assistant to help with the workload in the office. This would allow the team to stay in the field for longer periods. Danielle Cain became our anchor back home.

"Can I help?" I heard Dave's voice behind me but couldn't see him because I was overloaded with a stack of training manuals.

"Oh. Yeah – thanks."

I let Dave get the door and push the button for the elevator up. Once inside, he took some of the stack from me.

"What are these?" He asked.

"Training manuals to be redone." I pushed the number four.

"How is training going?" Dave asked.

"Good. Your lesson in pig farming really helped. Now that I understand we're moving sows, the implementations have gone so much smoother. And we have fewer sow effects."

I wasn't attempting to paint a pretty picture for Dave. Yes, we still had a problem here and there requiring some extra time but nothing overwhelming. This last training class was the first major problem we'd had in weeks.

The bell for the fourth floor rang and Dave and I exited the elevator.

"Here, let's put these in this conference room so I can spread out." I nodded towards an open conference room. Dave turned the light on with his elbow and we each put our stack on the table.

"The manuals were wrong?" Dave prodded.

"Not really wrong but not right. Anyway, it's not a big deal. It was frustrating for the class but it wasn't anyone's fault. Danielle put these together but she's new and didn't understand the process. The manuals are put together here then shipped to the facility. Each manual has the same core but specific pages are added for specific facilities. These were made with the right core but instead of the specific pages, all of the pages for all of the facilities were added. My flight got in late so I didn't have a chance to review them before class. When class started, I referred to certain pages. The pages weren't what they should've been and everyone got confused. I started to re-do them during class, but it got too complicated. I muddled through the class but I'm certain the people were irritated. I don't blame them. And it didn't help that a couple of high level managers were in the class."

"So you are going to re-do them yourself?" Dave prodded again.

"Yes, that way I know they're done right." I pulled the first manual and began to remove pages.

"Looks like a lot of work," Dave mused. "Do you have an instruction sheet for someone to follow?"

"Yes, I did but then that's how they ended up this way. Not a big deal, I'll just go through them myself." I wished Dave would just let this go.

Not likely. He grinned slyly, commenting, "Looks like you might've forgotten to include the details of pig processing."

"I think it's because she's new, that's all." I tried brushing it off hoping he'd see it my way.

"Yeah, that's what I thought but it really came back on me," said Dave.

"Okay, you win. I know that tone." I sat down, pushing the open manual aside, ready for another lesson in pig farming.

Dave sat down across from me. "Kate, you know I think you have the potential to be a good leader – that's why I share these with you."

"I know and I appreciate it." I knew he was sincere.

"Okay, I told you about moving sows and you've caught on quite well. You're going to be a pig farmer yet, Kate."

We laughed for a moment then Dave began. "You understand the importance of effective communication in the field but communication within your own group is equally important. I learned this a long time ago when a new employee started at the farm."

"Yven was new to the farrowing unit. He'd only been there about two weeks. This particular day, I was going to show him how to process pigs."

"See, within the first 24-48 hours of birth, pigs are handled for the first time. They have very small sharp teeth called milk teeth. These can be dangerous to the sow and to the other siblings so the sharp points are trimmed back. The pig is also given a shot of iron to help fight anemia. The entire process, when done correctly, takes only seconds per pig. With as many as 100 per day to be processed, you get pretty efficient at it."

"I showed Yven the technique a couple of times and asked if he understood. He nodded. I watched him process a couple. It was awkward for him just like it was for me when I first started so I wasn't concerned. Besides, I was in a hurry to get to other things. I patted him on the back and said I would be back to check on him. I went to another barn to do something else, confident he would handle the processing."

"After an hour or so, I began the trek back to the barn where he was working in. As I walked, I looked in the pens and noticed some of the newly processed pigs were standing in one spot, breathing hard. My pace quickened as I saw a few more pigs in this same condition."

"I caught up with Yven and pointing to one of the pigs, asked him what was happening. He was confused. He didn't see anything odd. Since he was new, he assumed it was normal. I had him show me exactly what he was doing. He picked up a pig and with one hand, held it around the girth. He then used his index finger to open the pig's mouth so he could clip the ends off the teeth. Just like I'd shown him. However, what he added to *his* technique was shifting his grip so now his middle finger was across the front of the pig's neck. Because he was new at processing, it was taking him much more than the typical few seconds per pig. This whole time, the pigs weren't able to breathe freely. The pigs I noticed were catching their breath!"

"I quickly pointed out what he was doing. We both felt awful. The pigs were fine but it was still an avoidable mistake. I took full responsibility for the mishap. I knew if I had taken the time to show him properly and watch his movements more closely before turning him loose, this wouldn't have happened. The price for my being in a hurry could have been very high."

Dave paused, thinking back for a moment before completing the lesson.

"Now that was the extreme Kate, and could have resulted in much greater loss than these mixed up training manuals. However, the point is the same. Vague instructions can cause real trouble. I'll bet if you look over your instructions, it'll be a list for you to follow, not for someone else to follow. To someone else, especially someone new, your instructions might be confusing. More likely, Danielle put them together exactly as you indicated. I'll also bet if you took a little time and went over the process with her again and this time, let *her* write the instructions, she'd get these manuals done in no time flat. Just as important, she'd be ready to prepare them correctly the next time."

"You and the rest of the team are getting stretched pretty thin here. I know you like things done your own way but you'll accomplish a great deal more if you learn to delegate and delegate effectively. As you become a leader, this will be critical to your success."

Dave was probably right. I remembered the day Danielle and I went over these manuals. I was rushing out the door to catch my plane.

I conceded. "I guess I was putting so much effort into moving sows, I didn't think to take the time with my own group."

"Good." Dave winked at me and got up, leaving the room.

I went back to my cube for a second to look at the instructions I made for Danielle. She had made a copy of the instructions, leaving me the original. I was embarrassed. Danielle had done the manuals exactly as I had indicated. The instructions failed to mention that the additional pages to add were different for each facility. She had no way of knowing the manuals were facility specific.

I found her and apologized for my haste and flawed directions. Together we went over the process again and this time, I included every detail. Free of the task of correcting the manuals, I was able to help Dave complete a presentation he was working on which included a progress report of the project. This was much smarter use of my time.

Later, back in my own cubicle, I added yet another lesson to remind me to slow down and give clear instructions:

Remember to Include the Details
of Pig Processing

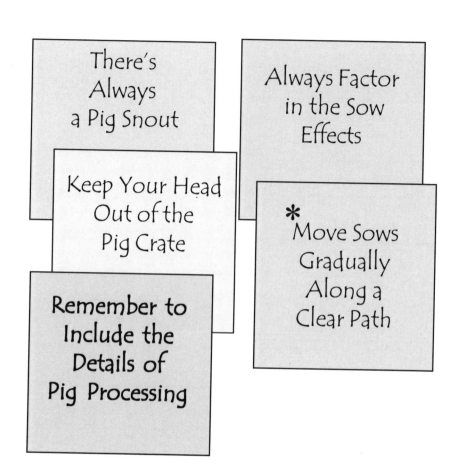

6

Never Trust the Boar

Boar – (noun) Bor 1: A male pig; 2: (slang) a person who will do anything to get ahead with little thought for anyone but him or herself

With the project running successfully at full throttle, I was rarely in the office. We had completed over half of the facilities and our team was beginning to get noticed by upper management.

Wednesdays at 9:00 am were marked as the weekly project update meeting. This week I was happy to participate in person rather than call in from the road.

The meeting was particularly upbeat. Much of this was because many of the large problems had been resolved and we could see the fruits of our efforts. It was also due in part to a new addition to the company, Tom Wade. Tom had joined the accounting team to help upgrade the accounting software. I liked Tom. He was positive and had a great sense of humor. He showed particular interest in the implementation of the purchasing project which I took as a compliment.

As the meeting ended, Tom followed me to my cube area so he could learn more. His questions were thoughtful and I felt comfortable letting him in on the successes as well as the failures.

After I showed him a demo of the software, he thanked me for my time and left. Dave saw him exit and scowled. I wondered what was up.

Dave leaned over, asking, "And what brought on Mr. Wade's visit?"

"Oh, he was interested in what we were doing and asked if I would show him more. He was really nice. I like him."

"Well, be careful Kate. The guy is a boar."

Without elaborating, Dave left and I didn't think much about it until weeks later.

I'd been traveling and unable to physically attend the next two meetings but was glad to be in the office this Wednesday so I could see everyone face to face. I waved to Tom as I entered the room. He waved back, smiling.

When it came time for my update, Tom stepped in, interrupting me a few times. I answered his questions but I began to get flustered. Tom continued his interruptions and went on further to point out all of the shortcomings, insinuating I had not addressed some of the issues.

I was humiliated. Tom would've never known these problems if I hadn't eagerly provided the information. And furthermore, all issues *were* being addressed despite his cutting remarks. I finished the last of my update and sat down seething.

When the meeting ended, I immediately took the opposite door, avoiding Tom. I knew I'd regret saying the sizzling words on the end of my tongue.

He caught up with me anyway, sliding the knife in further, stating cheerfully, "Great update, Kate!"

I resisted throwing my coffee in his face and turned away, claiming I had to use the restroom.

'Hey, don't take it personally, Kate. I just wanted to be sure everyone was aware of the challenges you were facing," his voice called to my back as I walked away.

Dave saw me stomp past his cube.

"Hey, hey, hey- what's happening?"

I pointed to the conference room knowing my voice would be hard to keep at a reasonable level. Dave met me there and closed the door. Not waiting for him to sit down, I regurgitated what happened, my voice clearly indicating how humiliated I was.

"And he only had that information because I gave it to him!" I yelled at Dave.

"Yes, a tried and true boar, Kate." Dave nodded and his voice sighed in exasperation. He went on.

"It doesn't surprise me. I worked with Tom before, and I know him. He did something similar to me when I was new to the company. He only thinks of himself, and he will do anything to anyone to make himself look good. Even if it means making your project look bad."

"I just wish I would've known. How did you know?" I asked.

"I know because I've been around the boars. Both here and on the pig farm. I learned on the farm not to trust them and I know now not to trust them here."

Dave pulled a chair out, beckoning me to sit. I obliged.

"On the pig farm, you know boars are mean just by looking at them. Here we don't necessarily have that advantage. The boars on the farm are in a nice roomy pen, and their sole purpose is to breed the sows. When the boar is needed, the boar handler carefully opens a series of gates so a path is made from the boar pen to the waiting sow."

"Boars don't move quickly and this gives the impression they are just moseying along, not paying attention to you. Don't be fooled. A boar *will* hurt you if it gets the chance. And they have a great sixth sense for the second you turn your back."

"We had a guy who'd been handling the boars for years. Never had a problem. He was careful. One day he was moving a big boar across the aisle to a breeding pen. The boar was making his way across the aisle, not even looking at the guy. Just about then, someone came through the door at the end of the barn and the boar handler turned his head to see who it was. In that instant, that old boar took a step forward and raked his nubby tusks across the back end of the guy and ripped a six-inch gash through his coveralls."

"That's how boars are, Kate. They're mean and they're sly."

I rolled my eyes. "Great – so this guy's going to take a chunk out of my hide?"

"No, it's not nearly as dramatic in corporate America but it is the same. Corporate boars will do anything to make themselves look good, often preying on those who never see it coming. They'll steal your ideas, take credit for your successes and blame you for any failures. In your case, Tom knows your project is going well, and his department isn't doing so hot. Rather than ask for your input, he makes you look bad so he looks better. And he's good at it- very smooth."

"What do you do about a boar?" I asked.

"For one, never trust the boar. Stay out of his way. If you try to go head to head with him, it'd be a losing battle. Just like you can't go head to head with a boar on the farm. That boar would slaughter you in a second. Be cordial to Tom but avoid him when you can. And don't give him any more information than he needs."

Dave paused then added with a wink, "The good news is, boars don't generally stay in the herd long."

I got his drift and went back to my cubicle. I had learned a good lesson here but was worried I'd forget it. To remind myself, I wrote in big block letters:

NEVER TRUST THE BOAR

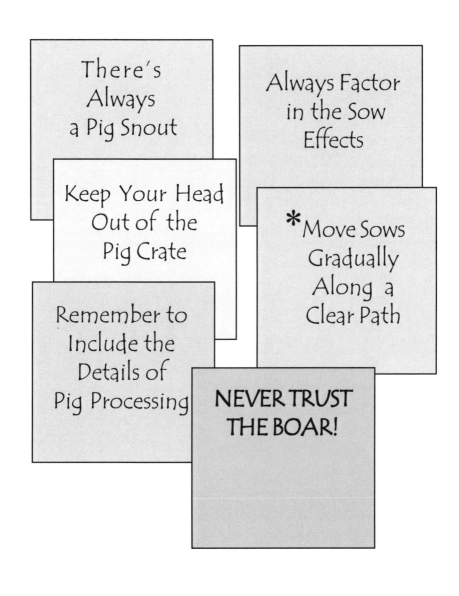

7

Hit Those Angry Sows Head On

Angry Sow – (noun) – ang' gree sow 1 : an agitated female pig; 2 : a customer, internal or external, who can enhance or dampen your career, depending on how effectively you resolve his or her problem

Heeding Dave's advice, I steered clear of Tom in the coming weeks, answering his emails cordially yet vaguely. Most of the time I was so busy, we didn't cross paths. The team continued its road show and we were pleased with how things were going. One Friday, I made it a point to get back to the office for at least one day to catch up on paperwork and to meet face to face with a few key people. It was always nice coming back to the office after a road trip. Hellos and welcome backs greeted me as I made my way to my cubicle with a fresh cup of coffee. I heard my phone ringing and quickened my pace to catch it.

"This is Kate." I answered.

"Kate, Bob White here. I'm the general manager at the Raton facility." His voice was deep and abrupt.

The hair on the back of my neck stood up and I resisted the urge to pretend he had reached my voice mail. Oh yes, I knew Bob. We had spent so much time at his facility, I was thinking about registering to vote there.

"Yes, Bob. How are things going?" I already knew the answer. Bob wasn't calling to chitchat.

"Not good Kate. That's why I am calling. Tom Wade and I have been talking, and well, Kate, I know you spent extra time but I still have issues not yet resolved. I am sending you an email today and copying your boss as well as a few others. I wanted to call and let you know so you wouldn't think I was blind-siding you."

I had to give him that. Many would have just sent the email. Besides, I knew the boar was egging him on.

"Is there something I can do?" I asked in hopes he would reconsider sending the email.

"Read the email. Many of these are issues I've brought up before. We just can't get this to work. Thank you Kate." He hung up.

I immediately searched my email, cussing Tom Wade under my breath. I knew there'd been many issues concerning Bob's facility but thought for sure they'd all been addressed. However, I also had to admit to myself that in some ways, I had avoided Bob because I figured, or more truthfully, *hoped* he would get used to the new system on his own. His facility had been one of the first to implement when there were still many problems with our process.

I didn't see Bob's new email yet so I printed the historical ones to refresh my memory. Bob opposed the new system from the beginning. His facility had implemented their own system several years ago and it was working just fine before we came into his facility and changed it. He had developed an easy rhythm using the reports from his system but was having a hard time adjusting to the new system's reports. I recalled spending extra training time to assist him and his staff. He'd also been concerned about his spend increasing because it appeared the new system had less controls. Several other issues were there.

I went to find Dave to warn him of the upcoming email. He was in his cube. Knowing the familiar beat of my footsteps, he didn't have to turn around to know it was me. He spoke while maintaining his focus on his computer screen.

"I thought you'd come by. I'm just reading the email."

"Oh, you got it? It wasn't in my mailbox yet but I thought I should let you know it was coming. Is it bad?"

I leaned over Dave's shoulder, reading the email. "Quite the pig snout, huh?" I asked, continuing to read.

"Oh, no, not the pig snout. This is much more serious. I see the boar is involved here but really, what we have here is an angry sow."

"I'm afraid to ask what that is. It doesn't sound good." I said as I leaned further in to hit the print button. "I'll be right back, Dave. I want to get hard copy then hear about this angry sow."

I perused the email again as I made my way back to Dave's cube. The system doesn't do this, it doesn't do that, it was much better the way it was before. In each case, he listed the problem and what he thought the solution should be. Some were possible and others were not. I noted he copied everyone but God and sat back down across from Dave.

Dave stretched then picked up the stack of emails I had brought over with me, sifting through them as he spoke.

"Yep, Bob is an angry sow. I know you spent a lot of extra time with his facility, Kate, but unfortunately, Bob has a lot of power here and with good reason -he's one of the best managers we have. But let's not fret too much and take a look at what we've got."

Dave reviewed each issue, periodically asking questions to make sure he understood the issue and why Bob's proposed solutions would or wouldn't work. After he reviewed everything, he sat back and summarized.

"The point Bob is making is that his old system was much better than the new system. And it probably was better - *for him*. But Bob's system isn't good for the whole company, and the whole purpose of this project is to standardize our purchasing system."

Dave slapped his hands on the tops of his legs. "The good news, as I mentioned before, is Bob *is not* a boar. He's reasonable and willing to change. He just wants to make sure he doesn't lose control in the process. I look at these issues and I think they're quite valid. I also know this. If we can resolve these issues to Bob's satisfaction, he'll be a strong advocate for the program."

"So what now?" I asked.

"Well, it may seem hopeless," Dave sighed. "But I learned a long time ago, the best way to deal with an angry sow is to hit her head on. Taka taught me this on the pig farm. I wouldn't have believed it unless I actually saw it."

I sat back in my chair and Dave spoke.

"We were moving sows one day. The last few sows were making their way to their crates, but this one sow was having a bad day and simply would not cooperate. We had the path well defined but she just decided she wasn't going in one of those crates. She reached one of our board walls and jumped clear over the top of it. When she landed, she lost her footing and stumbled a bit, but that just fortified her resolve. When she got her feet back under her, she started running at full speed straight down another aisle where two of the workers were standing. She was mad! I yelled for them to look out but it was too late. The first guy tried to steer her away but she head butted him like a bull tosses a cowboy and didn't lose a bit of momentum. She was now barreling full speed ahead towards Taka. Six hundred angry pounds of bacon heading for this little guy who's about 160 pounds after a big meal. I expected Taka to jump out of the way. Instead, he stood there, crouched down like an offensive linemen. I held my breath, waiting for her to level him."

"But then, the most amazing thing happened. Taka braced himself and just at the instant of impact, he hit that sow right back flat in the chest. This flipped her around 180 degrees and before she knew what happened, she was running in the other direction. I never would've believed it if I hadn't actually seen it! She grew tired a minute or two afterwards and we got her into her crate. Taka was fine and other than being shaken and a little bruised, the other guy was okay too."

"I talked to Taka about it and he told me in his English, 'Angry sow - hit head on! Her speed turn her around. She run other way.' And having just witnessed it, I believed him!"

Relating this back to the current situation, Dave went on.

"You need to do just what Taka did - hit this angry sow head on. Use the momentum of the problem to create a solution. You need to find the spot on Bob that'll flip him around and get him going where he needs to go."

Dave and I spent the next hour outlining each issue Bob's email had pointed out. After each one, we listed possible solutions or compromises. When no obvious solution was apparent, we listed appropriate questions to ask him to make sure we understood the issue. In many cases, Bob simply misunderstood a process or misinterpreted how the software worked.

I replied to his email the same day and while I was at it, scheduled a conference call with several key players to discuss possible solutions to Bob's dilemma. I phoned him several times before the call to see if any other issues had come up that should be included in the call.

After the conference call, I spent a few days at Bob's facility making sure new processes were understood. I also spent extra training time showing he and his associates how to run and read reports. In the end, Bob still would have preferred his own system, but he had a better understanding of the new system. I actually looked forward to talking with him rather than crawl underneath my desk as I had wanted to do weeks before.

Dave caught me on my cell phone while I was waiting for my flight back to the home office.

"Kate, I just wanted to let you know I was on a teleconference with Bob and a few of the other general managers today. Bob complimented you on your diligence in solving the problems. I can tell he's a lot more comfortable now. Good job Kate! That was quite an angry sow you turned around."

I thanked Dave and caught my plane home.

When I returned to work, I pulled the sticky note I had been carrying for support and added it to my whiteboard:

Hit Those Angry Sows Head On!

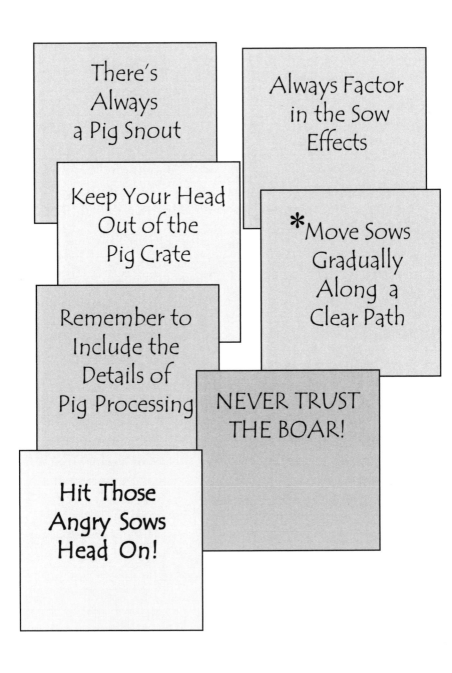

8

Heterosity is Vital For Continued Process Improvement

Heterosity (noun) - het·er·os'·i tee 1: the marked vigor or capacity for growth often exhibited by crossbred animals or plants; also called hybrid vigor 2 : (slang) the amount of freshness in a team or organization

Rounding the corner of my cubicle, I let my laptop sag to the floor before dropping an armful of files on my desk. Though it was a short walk, the weight of all my baggage made the trek from the car to my cube seem like a marathon. Massaging my arm to get the circulation back, I appraised the large stack of interoffice mail, wondering where to start.

I had just gotten back in town after three weeks in the field. We were pushing hard to complete the remaining 15 facilities.

Traveling was great when we first started. We had a rhythm to the work and were all enthusiastic. Morale was high and we all got along. But now I was tired. The entire team was tired.

I spotted Dave in the aisle headed in my direction.

"Hey, how's it going? Long time no see." Dave greeted me enthusiastically.

"It's going well." I responded, putting on my best 'I am the invincible corporate employee' face.

"The old traveling warrior with a laptop bit has lost some glamour for you, has it?" Dave saw through my efforts.

"No, really, we are making a lot of progress and I like it." I hated to be so tired.

"How many more facilities do you have to go?" Dave asked.

"Oh, I don't know, I lost count..." I sighed, revealing my weariness. Quickly recovering, I explained.

"Look, Dave. Don't get me wrong. I love what I do. I love this job and I love the team. We do a great job. It's just that in the beginning we were so fresh. We were new to each other. Our spirit and sense of humor were high. When things went wrong, one of us could always help the other one get back up. We're still efficient and get the job done, but I notice we have less tolerance for problems and for each other. I'll be fine – the team will be fine. We just need to regroup."

I sincerely smiled this time, already feeling better.

"Sounds like you need some heterosity." Dave said, nodding his head.

"Uh-oh, I feel the cobwebs lifting from my college biology. Is this another lesson in pig farming?" I teased him but I loved the lessons.

"Indeed it is, Kate. This is a good one! Grab a cup of coffee and meet me in the break room."

As soon as we were settled, Dave began:

"The birth of the pigs is a critical stage of the end product. Remember, the faster you can get a pig to 230 pounds, the faster you make money. The larger and the healthier pigs you get at birth, the easier it is to get pigs to grow to 230 pounds. Everyday, a fresh set of newborn pigs start this phase in the product cycle."

"When I first arrived at the farm, the newborn pigs were fat and healthy. After awhile, though, we noticed the newborn pigs weren't as large as they used to be. We also noticed more birth defects. Now, this didn't happen overnight. The changes were subtle, taking place so gradually you really didn't notice anything from day to day. Then one day, we saw it."

"What was happening was simple. We were losing heterosity - hybrid vigor. See, the best of the female pigs are kept for breeding. Inferior females and all of the males were sent to the pack house. When you plot that out over time, you can see it's possible that some of the females might have been bred to a boar they were related to. This creates a surplus of recessive genes, the weaker genes. This high number of recessive genes was causing lower birth weights and the increase in the number of birth defects."

"When we realized this, the farm boss headed for Dodge City, Kansas and bought new boars. The old boars were culled out of the herd and the new boars were put to work."

"Kate, you wouldn't believe the difference in that first crop of pigs fathered by the new boars. They were huge, robust buggers! Defects became almost nonexistent. It was incredible!"

Dave's hands spread apart, showing me how much bigger the new pigs were. Then he pointed, lowering his voice as if to reveal a secret.

"And it was the power of heterosity."

He paused before continuing.

"The same thing is happening to your team, Kate. You've been together for months, you've been on the road for months. Now you're tired. You need some new blood."

"What are you getting at!?" I asked warily, still unsure where he was going.

"No, Kate, I'm not saying this because I think you're doing a bad job or because I want to get rid of you or anyone else. What I *am* saying though is this is a good time to cross train the team. Danielle appears ready to move up. Add her into the mix so you can rotate the schedules for a while. This will add at least one fresh traveler to the team. Life is hard on the road- I know, I've been there. By introducing some new blood, you'll regain your enthusiasm. I'll also bet the whole team will improve. It's always beneficial to see and experience things on the other side. You'll each gain a better understanding of what everyone does."

He noticed the furrows in my forehead and tapped me on the arm to make sure I continued listening.

"And please don't take this personally, Kate. It's not just your team. This is normal. It's in every system everywhere. You see the reorganization going on here.

Everyday there's another email regarding a change. This isn't unique to our company. Every company everywhere is reorganizing. It's not that the leaders are doing a bad job. No more than those boars were doing a bad job. Heterosity is vital for continued process improvement in any organization. Large company, small retailer, pig farm, high tech computer manufacturer – every organization needs re-invigorating regularly. Heterosity is a powerful, necessary component. Trust me. A little bit of heterosity goes a long way."

After our meeting, our core team met to talk about possible changes. This was the home stretch and it was important to maintain our pace.

Danielle was added as part of the traveling team. Schedules were rearranged to give everyone a little more downtime in between trips. Danielle was happy to travel and experience the other side of the project. The rest of us were happy to get a longer reprieve from the road. Knowing we would have a break, our senses of humor returned. This would also give us a better understanding of each other's role. Enthusiasm was restored.

I could see heterosity already helping.

I added the lesson to my now nearly full whiteboard.

Heterosity is Vital For Continued Process Improvement

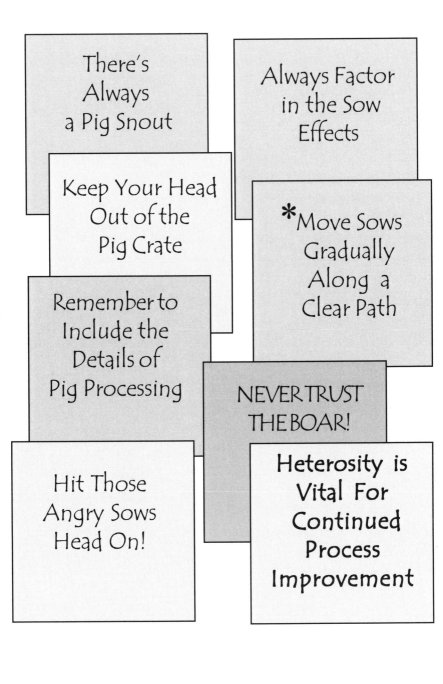

9

Know When to Let Go of the Nursery Pigs

"Although I'm always happy when I see a particularly difficult student get back on track, I do worry he or she will lose the momentum when they have to move to the next class. I need to learn to give them and me more credit than that."
                    -Kaiya Wolf, Special Education Teacher

The last push with renewed vigor really paid off. The last few months had been fun again. It was a nice way to end as a team. With just a few locations remaining, it was clear we no longer needed five people.

My three pod mates had been pulled to start or support other projects. Danielle and I remained. Danielle had come a long way from her first role as an administrative assistant.

At our weekly one-on-one, Dave and I went over the open items.

"Almost done, just two more to go and we're done. I can't believe it!" I was excited and sad all at the same time.

"Yes, this was a tough project, Kate. The rest get easier. You'll see." Dave closed his notebook.

The meeting was over but I had one more issue. I wondered if it was silly to bring it up. Dave caught me hesitating.

"What is it?" He asked.

I looked down, stuttered a bit, then began.

"Well…well, you know Danielle has been a big part of this project. She has helped out a lot and learned a lot. I know she's been looking at positions in other departments, but I feel like she would make a great administrator of this project. Someone has to stay on to continue to manage the day-to-day stuff. It would be a nice step up for her."

"Does she want to stay on as the administrator?" Dave asked.

"I don't know. I guess. I kind of feel like I mentored her and it'd be a great move for her." I kept my voice noncommittal, hoping he would agree.

"And you could continue to mentor her, even from a distance, right?"

Dave knew me well. Though I hadn't yet admitted it to myself, this *was* the reason.

"Yeah, I guess." I paused, now embarrassed. "I guess I'll just hate to see her go if she moves to another project. Everyone loves her and she's very talented."

Dave nodded. "That she is, Kate, and don't sell yourself short on that one. You helped her blossom. She's one of your brood, so to speak. I know exactly what you mean."

Dave laid his palms across the arms of his chair, tapping twice. "Yes, it's important to know when it's time to let go of the nursery pigs."

Dave checked his watch and asked me. "Do you have time for this?"

I smiled. "I always have time for your lessons in pig farming, Dave."

"Good. " Dave responded. "I think you'll like this one."

Dave began.

"Part of my job on the farm was to take care of the sick pigs in the nursery. When pigs are weaned from their mothers, they're moved to the nursery. This was a large room divided into eight pens, four on each side. The 600 or so pigs weaned each week are sorted according to size

93

and weight. Larger pigs with larger pigs, and smaller pigs with smaller pigs and so on."

"At the end of the sorting, there'd be ten or 12 pigs that were so small they had to be put in special 'baby' crates. These were like little playpens set off the ground in the two front pens. One or two pigs would be put together. Here they could be coddled along until they were big and strong enough to go back in the herd. These pigs are fed high calorie diets, usually sweetened to be more palatable. Like a pediatric unit in pig farming."

"This was my favorite part of my job. I hand fed many of the pigs, taking it as a personal challenge when one of the pigs wouldn't eat. Call it maternal instinct. I would crumble cookies in milk, mix Jell-O and oats, combine chocolate milk with corn meal– anything to get those little pigs to eat. After a few days, the pigs would recognize me. They'd squeal in anticipation when I entered the barn with the day's entree. I loved it."

"After a few weeks, the pigs were healthy and plump. The high calorie diet and personal TLC paid off. I however, was in denial. In taking care of those little pigs, nurturing them, getting them back on track, I had gotten attached to them and didn't want to let them go. As they grew larger and took up more space in their small pens, I refused to notice."

"It was Taka who brought me back to reality one day. He waited while I fed the pigs, now big and healthy and obviously out of space in their undersized roomettes. When I finished feeding, Taka called me over and placed a hand on my shoulder and said, 'You like baby pig. They need you. You like a Mama. You like that.'"

"And I did like it so I nodded in agreement, smiling proudly as their 'Mama.'"

"Taka continued, saying, 'Pigs better now, they grow up-ready to leave small pen. They not need Mama. You need to let go.'"

"And you know, Kate. Taka was right. I had focused on my own satisfaction and was avoiding letting them go, despite their obvious need to move on."

"The next day Taka and I moved the pigs in with the rest of the herd. I had to remind myself of this lesson for the remainder of my days at the farm. I still took it as a personal challenge to help these little pigs along, and I still got attached. But I also knew when it was time to let go."

Dave shifted in his chair then resumed.

"Kate, when you have to say good-bye to one of your employees who has outgrown a position, it feels the same way. You have been Danielle's 'Mama' so to speak. She started out here as an administrative assistant and you worked with her, gave her direction and helped her through the tough spots. Now she is ready for more challenge.

That's the sign of a good leader Kate, when you can expand a person's skill set so they can move beyond where they would be had they just been on their own."

"The second part of being a good leader is knowing when to let go like I had to learn when it came time to let go of the nursery pigs."

Dave paused for a moment then said very softly.

"Just as I know what I'll feel when you move on to your next challenge."

We both smiled then, a bit self-consciously. I was grateful to have Dave as a leader.

We left the conference room and I went to my cube.

Days later, Danielle approached me and told me she was applying for a position with another company altogether. Although she had loved this position, she wanted more challenge.

As I wrote her recommendation, I glanced up at the whiteboard, my attention focused to the latest edition:

Know When to Let Go of the Nursery Pigs

I was sincerely happy for her, and knew she'd do a great job for her new company.

10

In the End, it's All Just Pig Farming

"Live for today."
-Pops

Intensely engrossed in my work, I hadn't noticed Dave walk up behind me.

"Hey," he said.

I jumped, startled by his voice.

"Oh, didn't mean to scare you." We both laughed. Dave pulled up a chair from the neighboring desk.

"What time is it?" I asked. "And what are you doing here?"

Dave rarely stayed past six. I glanced at the lower right of my screen. It was 8:57.

Shrugging, Dave said, "Oh, I forgot my wallet and besides, I just wanted to make sure everything was ready for the move tomorrow."

"Oh that's right. You get the big cube now – got a table and everything. You're moving up town." I ribbed Dave.

We both chuckled then looked away from each other. The mention of the move made things awkward for a moment.

An unannounced reorganization changed a few things. The home office was being downsized to meet the new budget. Some of the home office staff went to the field facilities but many were laid off.

"You heard about Tom Wade, right?" I asked. "He's going to work for Bob White."

Dave smiled, nodding. "Yeah, I expect he'll bounce a few more times before he finally leaves. I told you boars don't stay in the herd long."

"And Greg took a position with a consulting company," I reported. We both grinned recalling Greg's zeal for saving those millions. He'd do great there.

Of my three former pod mates, two had been laid off, but one would become the administrator of the purchasing program.

I thought back over the last year. Hard to believe it had actually been a whole year. It felt like only a few months.

Thankfully, Dave had been moved to a Director position. I was happy for him. Of all the people I'd known here, he deserved it.

The re-org meant good things for me as well. I would now be a Team Leader with a staff of two, and of course, a single, larger cube. Unfortunately, I would no longer report to Dave.

"I'll miss you and your lessons in pig farming," I pointed to my white board. The splotches of colored sticky notes and scraps of paper were now replaced with a neat list of nine lessons.

"I'll miss you too." Dave responded, speaking softly and shifting in his chair. "But I'm sure we'll cross paths again. Small world out there."

We were both silent for a moment. Dave broke the silence by commenting, "I've noticed you've been working late a lot."

Glancing toward my computer I answered, "Just a lot to finish before the changeover. I'm almost done."

Dave shook his head from side to side. "Kate, through all my lessons in pig farming, I really thought you'd get it."

"Get what?" I asked.

He hesitated then was silent again. I knew that look. "Oh, is this my final lesson in pig farming from the great porcine prince?" I prompted him.

Dave looked up laughing, pulled his chair in close, pointing his index finger at me and said, "Yes. Yes it is, Kate. And this is the most important lesson of all."

I turned my chair to face him. "Then do tell, great corporate swine farmer."

Dave began.

"Kate, not all lessons in pig farming involve pigs. I worked with many great people, and they all taught me something. But this one guy Pops taught me the most important lesson of all."

"Pops was 76 years old when I arrived at the farm. He was responsible for welding damaged crates back together. He was a small man, no more than five six and weighing 150 or so. His head was bald except for the outcrop of several gray hairs and a speckling of age spots. He wore heavy, black-rimmed glasses with thick lenses. But even through those, you could see the sparkle in his eye. He wasn't very talkative but when he did speak, we all listened. He was always soft spoken and gentle. He'd listen to us talk about our dreams and what we were going to do when we got rich. He'd lift his leathery finger and point to us saying, 'Live for today,' the whole time smiling like he was hiding some delicious secret."

"Pops did have a bit of a wild streak in him. I had the opportunity to experience this first hand when I drove to the barns with him one morning. I was looking forward to a slow drive down the dirt path - not at all eager to dive into the day. Boy, was I shocked! I got in the passenger side of that '57 rusted Chevy truck, barely closing the door when Pops hit the gas pedal and we were gone. My head flew back then to the side as Pops turned the first corner at what felt like 50 miles per hour. I swear we were on two wheels."

"Pops hit the brakes with the same aggression as the gas, nearly knocking my teeth out against the dash as we pulled up to the barn. It was then that I thought I understood the sparkle in his eye. I had no doubt he had been a wild one in his younger years."

"I admired Pops. I assumed he was widowed and wanted something to do. He welded, joked with us and passed along his words of wisdom."

"One day, while working on a crate, Pops had a heart attack and had to be rushed to the hospital. We were all worried sick. He was the farm favorite by a long shot. The lunchtime chatter was all about Pops and what would happen. Still under the assumption Pops didn't have to work, I asked why Pops just didn't retire and kick back rather than continuing to work so hard. The room fell silent for a minute. Then, in a very low tone one of the barn managers said softly, 'Pops has to work. He needs the money.'"

"I was dumbfounded by his answer. It was so far from what I'd thought. But by then it was time to go back to work so I didn't get the whole story. Within a week, Pops returned to the farm and life returned to normal."

"Many months later, the Farm Boss and I flew to Dodge City, Kansas to get new boars. He had his own plane, a small two-seater, twin engine job. It was a long ride so after exhausting our business chatter, I asked him about Pops and he shared Pop's story with me."

"Pops lived in the same small town all his life. In high school, Pops met a girl, and she was *the* girl for Pops. He fell madly in love and it wasn't long before she felt the same way. They were both wild spirits. Good-natured wild spirits, not bad or mean. Both of them were well known in the community."

"After they graduated from high school, they married, and moved to a small home. They both loved to bowl. Every Wednesday and Friday, you could catch them in action at the local bowling alley. They were always surrounded by lots of laughter, friends, and playfulness."

"Several years into their marriage, they decided if they could build up enough money, they could retire early and spend their golden years traveling the world. Both of them had been in the same little town their whole life and they were anxious to see what was out there."

"They each had steady jobs, and in addition to that income, they bought fixer-upper houses. Side-by-side they worked day and night to repair them, dress them up, then sell them for a profit. All of the profits went into their 'golden year fund.' By the time they reached their mid-50's, they realized they'd saved quite a bit of money and began planning their retirement."

"And they did it. By the time they were 60, both were retired. They decided to hang loose around town for a while since they hadn't had much time to enjoy life there while working so hard for so many years. They spent six months or so bowling, going to the drive-in, playing cards and socializing with friends."

"It wasn't long after this that Pops's wife began to forget things. Not big things but little things. She might lose her car keys or forget someone's name. At first it wasn't a big deal but as it got worse, she got frustrated. Pops worried too but they both figured it was just a part of getting older."

"One night Pops and his wife arranged to meet at the bowling alley at eight o'clock. Pops arrived first and talked with friends while he waited. When it got to be eight-thirty he started to worry. When the clock turned past nine, Pops called the sheriff and jumped in his own truck to start looking for her."

"It was the sheriff who found her. She was two blocks from the bowling alley, parked on the side of the road, leaned over her steering wheel crying. She explained through tears that she couldn't find the bowling alley and she couldn't remember how to get home."

"Pops arrived shortly after and took her home. Her condition could no longer be ignored."

"Just before her 62nd birthday, Pops's wife, his mate of over 40 years, was diagnosed with Alzheimer's. Sometimes the disease progresses slowly, sometimes quickly. For Pops's wife, it went quickly. Soon, she had to be put in a convalescent home because Pops could no longer keep her safe from herself. Pops got her in the best home available, barring no expense. Years went by and their 'golden year' funds dwindled."

"The Farm Boss explained to me that Pops visited his wife every day for the past 15 years though she had long ago forgotten who he was. He'd hold her hand and touch her face as gently and as lovingly as he had when they first met years ago. They were still together, but they spent their golden years in very different worlds."

"Kate, at the time I was on the farm, Pops was 76 and his wife was still alive. Pops continued working so he could eat and pay utilities, saving his other funds to continue his wife's care. I now understood the deep meaning of Pops' wise words 'Live for Today.' It wasn't some delicious secret but a cover for a deep regret."

Dave and I sat in silence for a few minutes. I didn't know what to say. Dave finally spoke.

"Kate, it isn't often I'm in the office late but when I am, I notice the other folks around me. There's Ken who has a wife and three kids who I bet he hasn't had dinner with in years. There's Becky who seems to live here, bypassing her youth looking through pounds and pounds of data. Lisa spends four days on the road and one in the office, coming in many weekends to catch up. She just got married last year."

"I used to catch myself feeling the need to finish one more thing. But then I recall Pops' finger pointing at me, his voice echoing, 'Live for today' and know he's right. No matter how carefully we plan, or how hard we work, or how much we hope and wish for, life could change at any moment."

"And Kate, this was the greatest lesson in pig farming. *Balance* your life. Work hard but play hard. Keep your family and the time you spend with them your highest priority in life. Today may be all you have. Keep your perspective on what's important. The work can wait – there'll be plenty of it tomorrow. In the end, it's all just pig farming."

We sat for a moment longer before Dave pushed himself up from the chair.

"Come on – let's get out of here." Dave motioned towards the door.

I shut down my computer, grabbed my coat and started to follow him.

"Oh wait, just a sec." I turned back to my cube. Grabbing a pen from the desk, I wrote at the bottom of my list:

In the End, it's All Just Pig Farming

Lessons in Pig Farming

There's Always a Pig Snout

Keep Your Head Out of the Pig Crate

Always Factor in the Sow Effects

Move Sows Gradually
Along a Clear Path

Remember to Include the
Details of Pig Processing

Never Trust the Boar

Hit Those Angry Sows Head On

Heterosity is Vital For
Continued Process Improvement

Know When to Let Go
of the Nursery Pigs

*In the End, it's All
Just Pig Farming*

Acknowledgments

First and foremost, much appreciation goes to Terry Carr. I could not have done this without his endless support. (If he's reading this, I know he's shaking his head). It's true. If it hadn't been for his tenacious prodding, this would have still been an idea I was kicking around. His belief in me kept me going; his sense of humor kept me from getting too serious. Thank you, thank you, thank you!

Thanks to Anita Collins, my first real reader, "editor" and cheerleader. Thanks for all your help and support! Kaiya Wolf, real life angel, best friend, and life teacher. Jim and Cindy Runner, the greatest friends and brainstorming buddies anyone could ask for. Trina Bain for reading (and re-reading) and constant support both with the book, with work,and with life. Jeanne Peroglio, Dan Munson, Virginia Ford, and Dale Folsom - all anchors in my life who remind me of who I am when I forget. John Nyheim, for keeping the household under control when I became submerged in this project. (Tessie and Callie thank you too!)

Many thanks to Toastmaster's International, specifically the Palm Lane group. The enthusiasm and support of this organization is boundless. Special thanks to Donna Davis and Nancy Krause.

Thanks to Greg Catt, Doug Gauger, Roberta Hacker, Jessica Kephart, David Stenz, Robyn Szurgot, Fran Yurick, the rest of the SBS gang and all of the others who offered enthusiasm and support along the way. Special thanks to Marcia Jones and Dan (Dan-O) McNamara.

Long overdue thanks to Judith Rumohr, Mrs. Woodall, and Mr. Mahn; all phenomenol teachers who changed my life forever and who I'm certain, continue to make the world a better place. And finally, sincere thanks to everyone at Gilt Edge Farms for teaching me all about pig farming.

About the Author

Cathy Sumeracki worked on a large commercial swine operation just after graduating from Michigan State University.

For the last 15 years, Cathy has worked in various large, multi-facility companies where she has been closely involved in the implementation of new purchasing programs.

She continues her role in change management working in Arizona.